JUST ONE SWALLOW

Laura P. McCarty

A NOTE FROM THE SELECTOR

This manuscript was selected for publication from among a group of exceptional books submitted for consideration by past finalists of Day Eight's DC Poet Project competition. When I was asked to be the selector I didn't assume I would have as strong a group to select from as I did, or that such an extraordinary book would be among the applicants.

Laura McCarty's Just One Swallow gracefully navigates the brutal and beautiful (sometimes in the same poem; occasionally the same line), often on the verge of revelation or else doubling back to track the wreckage. This collection provides a guided tour of her past and present: a daughter, a mother, a traveler, a restless soul in search of feelings attainable only via honesty and experience.

Featuring a more analog America readers of a certain age will remember, and remote locales rendered at once exotic and unadorned, here are words you can taste, views you can smell, and portraits you can inhabit. Depicting the '70s, the South, the pleasure and pain of sexual awakening, bucolic landscapes, and domestic battlegrounds, this work is a sustained shout in defiance of dark and silent spaces.

A good poet is able to explore feelings through images that resonate as universal or self-evident truths; an exceptional poet–like McCarty–manages to turn observations into epiphanies one is grateful to obtain, and share.

Sean Murphy
Executive Director
1455: A Place for Writers

ADVANCE PRAISE FOR JUST ONE SWALLOW

Laura McCarty, storyteller, is a credit to the narrative tradition; and has no superior. Her debut book is astonishing reading: each poem is brought home with new breath and surprise; each page is more powerful than the last, giving language the courage it deserves. One of McCarty's characters 'sticks her fingers through the wire/ shaped like steel diamonds.' That could describe this collection–truth cut hard, brilliance.

–Grace Cavalieri, Maryland Poet Laureate

The power of poetry is how it becomes a vessel for the silence one struggles to give voice to. There is no consent here. Only after the domestic secrets are undressed and the scars revealed can the reader go outside with this poet to sunny days and motherhood and maybe see the Buddhist monks walking.

–E. Ethelbert Miller, Host of On the Margin (WPFW 89.3 FM)

Often impactfully sparse in their sensorial landscapes, these poems dance with crisp imagery and graceful, well-crafted lines. McCarty's knack for portraits is especially evident in "Sister Bay, Wisconsin," the account of a drowning. Elsewhere, McCarty chronicles incidents of sexual abuse and rape with poised detachment. A memorable first book.

–Naomi Ayala

Like memorable fragments of conversation overheard on a train, Laura McCarty's poems are compelling and intriguing. Just One Swallow delivers cogent observations of a woman's life lived in a wide array of settings, and rewards the reader with the desire for more.

–Beth Joselow

From the first pages of McCarty's tremendous debut, Just One Swallow, we witness the conditioning of young women in "Switches," a masterful poem about the consequences of a small rebellion against the state. I am reminded of the poetry of Randall Jarrell, his ball turret gunner, who speaks out from the world of the dead against the indoctrination of the living. Here, the story of containment and curtailment of women's lives is carried by a gifted poet's language, and it all has to do with a final refusal to submit or consent to the abuses of a toxic, male-oriented society. The triumph of McCarty's poetry begins in the early recognition that this speaker and her sisters "belong to [the] mother's land," and this seed of awareness grows to sequoia size through the journeys herein, from the sprawling West, to far off encounters abroad, and home again to the Texas Hill Country where the book begins. There is a spiritual journey going on before our eyes, in which the speaker implicates and releases herself, and where the movement is really inward and backward rather than outward, back to the source of all comforts, the beloved green dress sewn by the mother. The last poems, down to the final lines of this book, are some of the finest I have ever read to complete a collection of poetry.

–David Keplinger, author of The Long Answer: New and Selected Poems

A splendid read. Absorbing Laura McCarty's poetry is like watching a Jungian dream unfold, she seems to be all the characters at once–a multi-level kaleidoscope of feeling, of what it means to be human–the joy from pain, the pain from joy. It isn't often I can't wait for the next poem or, for that matter, read a poetry volume straight through. This is one of those times.

–Elizabeth Hodges, Editor/Publisher, St. Petersburg Review and the Springhouse Journal

ACKNOWLEDGMENTS

My deep appreciation goes to my poetry teachers David Keplinger and Kyle Dargan. Their kindness, encouragement, mentorship, and wisdom were invaluable in the crafting of this book. Thanks also to my poetry workshop colleagues and my mother who have endured early versions of many of these poems and whose feedback made them better.

This book would not have been completed without the generosity of Day Eight, the encouragement of Robert Bettmann and the eye of my editor Anne Becker. Thank you.

My sincere thanks to the editors of the following publications and outlets, where these poems first appeared, sometimes in different versions.

descant–"Vicuña"
Jelly Bucket–"Switches"
Poetry Super Highway–"Buffalo Bayou"
St. Petersburg Review–"Those Woods"
Written in Arlington–"The Rut"

Finally, my limitless love and gratitude go to my daughters, Chloe and Cynthia, and to my mother. I love you.

Just One Swallow

For my mother
and my daughters

Table of Contents

Black-eyed Susans crumple over

THE HOME WE WILL REMEMBER

I am born in the black hills of eastern Kentucky
to a young woman from the Gulf Coast of Texas
who sews matching dresses for her three daughters
and sings at church to the kind of God that requires
service Sunday, Monday, Tuesday, Wednesday,
Thursday, Friday, and the occasional Saturday.

She weeds clover out from under her
orange blossoms, watches her pregnant neighbor
eat paint chips from her window sill
and listens to Rachmaninoff. Appalachia's blue ash
and accordions are not my mother
who grew up picking cotton, a penny a pound.

She begs my father to leave. He doesn't.
For a while. In a tan VW bug
with a diaper pail swishing in the back,
ammonia wafting, my mother drives us away
from the Ashland hills to the home
we will remember, where alligators live

in the swamp near the public swimming pool,
the garbage truck will save us from a four-foot flood,
and my sister will collect tarantulas with broken legs.
We will hide in bathtubs from tornadoes
and water our house in droughts
to keep from losing the foundation.

My sisters and I were birthed in the hollers
but our bodies know
the salt marshes, big sky, and green lizards.
We belong to our mother's land,
its tortillas and fried catfish,
its beaches and its air.

SWITCHES

My sister Cathlene stood on the air conditioner
her white nightgown fluttering from the fan,
a crown of blue bonnets in her hair.
We cheered for her like she was Jesus.

Liz and I, the thieves who hung by her side,
picked the state flower, knowing it was a crime.
Father let us choose our own switches
from the backyard. Mom grew roses.

We leaned over the hurricane fence and stole
the neighbor's witch hazel branches. Thick was better
than thin. Proud of our choices, we walked behind
the garage, handed over the winning picks

and lifted our gowns.

THE GREEN GRASS SNAKE

Dad chopped the head off the green grass snake
with the flat blade shovel he found in the garage.
Liz thought it was the garden hose we used to cool
the sidewalk when we jumped rope in our bare feet.

Red on yellow, kill a fellow. Red on black, won't kill Jack.
We knew this snake that lived in the garden
with the watermelons we grew. We had no rhyme
to keep it safe. I was six, my sister was eight.

When the screen door slammed, we knew dad was coming.
So we hid. He held the shovel down until the head came off.
Mom, hands on her hips, watched him bury the head
because snakes can bite you long after they're dead.

HOUSTON MASSACRE

In the mornings, my sisters and I hunted
for night frogs that climbed their way up
from the bayou to Mr. Patel's 7-11 parking lot
searching for dry land, crumbs from trash cans

or maybe new breeding grounds, smashed by
the mother running out for milk late at night,
crushed by the teenager cruising for a smoke
or a truck driver needing a Coke.

Mr. Patel paid us, the neighborhood cleaning crew
25 cents a day to scrape up the dried
flattened frogs with tire tracks imprinted
on their backs, baked stiff from the heat.

We flung them to the boys across the street.
They collected frogs, too, live ones they used
for target practice with their BB guns.
Pop. Pop. Pop. We weren't like them,

but we watched.

1976

Mr. Patel's 7-11 – a daily ritual
the summer Mom went to work.
In the afternoons, my sisters and I
walked to his store. When we thought
he wasn't looking, we stole Milky Way bars.
He never called the police, only our mom.
The phone rang until he let us go.
Thieves like Nixon, he'd say.
We knew then we were free.
Sometimes, he let us keep the candy.
We cartwheeled our way down
to the bayou behind the store.
There we played in the cattails and licked
the melted chocolate from the wrappers.
Later we climbed back up the hill
and waved to Mr. Patel through the window.
Don't leave those wrappers
on the ground! he yelled
banging on the window from the inside.
Never, Mr. Patel. We threw the wrappers
in the sewer and watched to see
if they grew up to be candy bar trees.
We got good at watching that summer.
The Olympics were on TV.
We all three believed
we could be Nadia Comaneci.
We wore our red, white, and blue bodysuits,
walked on broken logs across the swamp water,
pretended to be on the balance beam.
Stick your chest out and throw your arms up
in a Victory V, my sister Cathy ordered.
It was the year of freedom, the year my mom
walked into the kitchen and told my dad
she was leaving him. My dad was cooking bacon,

making his famous orange-flavored biscuits.
He threw the water meant for the biscuits
into the bacon grease and blew his hands up
like a grenade in a kitchen fire. We watched
his flesh bubble and brew, his fists clenched,
arms waving in the air, screaming at our mother.

THOSE WOODS

My little brother ran away on a duped-up Schwinn
to the dirt bike paths in the woods behind our school.
I knew where to find him but didn't go looking

in those woods, where my sister and I shoot
the moon on our roller skates, down rocky
hills that scrape off our skin, leaving us

with raspberries we hide from our father.
Those woods where we swing on the willow
branches, our weight stripping every leaf as we do.

Where my best friend Rochelle and I study
her mom's *Joy of Sex,* trying out the positions
with our clothes on and grading each other.

Those woods where Mike B. chased me after school
knocked me to the ground and kissed me
because he thought I'd like it. I was 10.

I found the neighbor molesting my friend in those woods.
Everything I saw was my fault not his, he said,
because I forgot to whistle to announce my arrival.

Those woods where my sister's friends let me try
pot from an apple pipe we dug out with a pen.
Where Billy, Johnny and I hit golf balls

until one ricocheted back into Billy's head.
That summer when my father was beating up my brother
I let him run away because he could.

MY FATHER TOLD ME TO BE HIS PILLOW

like I was a fluff of duck feathers,
his head heavy on my stomach,
until he traded me for a sister
if I breathed too big or squirmed.

TWO PENNIES

In heels and giant clip-on earrings,
Lucy Lee wore a net over her hair
to keep the curl while she served eggs.
We played at the booth with the orange seat,
the one ripped and pouring yellow
stuffing. Beneath the table we piled
bowls of food as high as we could.
We found pennies and hid them in our pockets
while our grandmother waited on men.
At night, Granddaddy Mac picked us
up in Lucy Lee's army-green Pontiac.
He moved over so she could drive.
In back, our bodies winged from side to side
as she took the corners. Windows open,
cigar smoke flying, Mac promised us
two pennies if we hung out the window
and caught the smoke in our mouths.

THE FIRST TIME I MET MY STEP-FATHER HE SHOWED ME A POLAROID OF HIMSELF STANDING NEXT TO A GIANT OSTRICH AND SWORE THE WALKING BIRD WAS HIS PET OSCAR

I was seven when this Greek New Orleans man
with a Cajun drawl rolled up into the driveway
in a turquoise Cadillac. He got out of the car
licking his powdered-sugar fingers and started
passing out beignets from a brown paper bag.
One week later he bought a freezer for our kitchen
packed it with Twinkies and Suzy Q's and told us
to never ask again if we could have dessert.
His name was Art and my sisters and I called him that,
which seemed like playing hooky and getting
away with it. We left the formalities of *yes, sir*
and *may I* with our mother's first husband.
The belt got put away, the switches stayed on the bushes.
He took us out of Texas to a mansion in upstate New York.
When we had to move again, he bought us
a Newfoundland puppy on our drive to Chicago.
With our car loaded with kids and suitcases, we squeezed
"Sweetheart" in. Our first dog. She was our lollipop.
We took road trips to Wall Drug in South Dakota.
I learned how to fish at five o'clock in the morning,
replaced Spam and hominy for bacon-wrapped
shrimp and Baked Alaska. He said the sun was shining
when it was raining, and we could only believe him.

PACT

The Greyhound bus
pointed us
toward yellow mountains,
bison on the roadside
and more sky
than we could swallow,
as we made a pact
to suck on silver dimes
until our skin turned blue.
We punctured our arms
with No. 2 pencils
and attached clothespins
to our necks.
We had all of Colorado
and Nebraska
to forget about
our father's new baby,
the one he named
Kathlene, with a K.
Every hour we traveled,
my sister Cathlene, with a C,
paid me a quarter
to let her bite my knee
with the promise that
I'd only bruise not bleed
as we moved down the highway
away from him.

OUT OF TEXAS

I drive away
from the cedar
the grackles
and prickly pear–
out of the desert
away from locust
shedding on my window sill.
I leave the sticker bushes
fire ants and cockroaches,
say goodbye to the sun
that frizzles my skin.
I crawl across
Louisiana, Alabama,
Georgia, the Carolinas,
and Virginia,
to the District of Columbia.
1,500 miles from home,
I can hear my mother's
garbled tongue.
She's hemming my Easter dress
when I am three
straight pins in her mouth,
la la la-ing to Mephistopheles.
How does she not swallow
the pointed metal? The colored
heads bob up and down as she
demands of me to "sand sell".

waterworn

HEAVIER THAN WATER

All bodies sink   my mother warned   stay close to shore

largemouth bass   those opportunity eaters   feed on

the bottom   if I could I would   hibernate with frogs

who hide in the mud   washed down from the stream

scraping over broken rocks   my mother warned

you will swim with the dead   do they see you

the lake's secrets wash up   when the moonlight leaks

pelicans plunge   birds have a third eyelid to see

frogs breathe through their skin   underwater

it's impossible to sing

SISTER BAY, WISCONSIN

The waves capsized
Steven and David,
lifted them up,
pulled them down,
filled their mouths
until they sank.
For thirty days,
the brothers settled–
bodies of water–
into the lakebed.
The boys' mother
wore an orange
life vest to garden
as if they would rise
up from dry land.
She was ready
when her sons
floated to the air
bloated beyond
recognition,
waterworn.
Both washed up
on the same day,
scattered on
the shore not far
from each other.

MONTICELLO

To Sally Hemings

After the house tour, the young girl
and her father walked the rolling green lawns,
stopping briefly on Mulberry Row
to see where you lived.
                                        They moved
toward the canopy of trees that shaded
them from the June sun. He picked her
up by the ribs and placed her
                                        on the stone wall,
its jagged edges poking the underneath
of her thighs. If she reached up
she could have grabbed the hanging
Marseilles figs. Instead, she watched
                                        its sugar drip
down onto her legs.
He opened them—gently tracing
the stitching of her jeans. When he
reached the end, she turned her head
toward the lane.

NO CONSENT

When he asked me to dinner I didn't know I could say anything
but yes when he said his friend would tag along, I thought
he was showing me off, he walked me to a motel room, shattered
its window, told his friend to keep watch, grabbed me
by the wrists and pulled me in, scraping my belly against glass,
I didn't scream because I was afraid I would get in trouble
for trespassing and worried he thought I was fat because
he couldn't get my jeans all the way off. I wanted him to like me,
so he would stop.

ACCOUNTING

WHO	WHERE	WHEN
home exterminator	My basement	2011
work colleague	In the back of a 4x4 on a highway in the Dominican Republic	2010
dermatologist	His office–Arlington, Virginia	2009
employer	In a parking lot	2008
first date	Fort Lauderdale, Florida	1986

WHAT HE DOES	WHAT HE SAYS
Traps me against my washing machine	I made you a mixed tape.
Leans across me, pressing his arm into my chest to open the opposite window.	I want to dance with your breasts.
Drops packets of Retin-A at my feet, bends down and looks up my dress. My eight-year-old daughter sits next to me. We are there for her skinrash, not my face.	I can get you lots of those eye packets for free if we are good friends.
Grabs my arms. I turn my face. His 80-year-old wet lips miss mine. My cheeks are soaking as if a dog has licked them.	See you tomorrow.
Breaks into a hotel room. Rapes me.	You'll be a good mother someday.

I SWALLOWED GOD WHOLE

mouth open, tongue out
the way Crystal
drank the lake.
Her dress floated
until she began to sink.
I am not in a state of grace
but clamp my jaw shut
on the priest's fingers
then turn my back
on the two-foot, artisan-crafted
red oak coffin.
I slide back into the pew
next to my kneeling husband
who spits his grief.

THE WIND IN OUAGADOUGOU

Monsoons demand all the senses. The cacti
in the planters shudder as if wishing me to stop.
My clothes are heavy with sweat, and a sweet smell
of roasting peanuts drifts over. A purple sky flies
toward me, the wind lifts up the city's few trees
like an offering and wrought-iron gates bend.
I dance in the Sahel under Christmas lights
on a garden patio. I dance to forget about the boy
pushing his nearly-dead cow in a wheelbarrow
to sell at the market, the girl whose face could not
be recognized–her mother knew her from the mole
on her inner thigh. The cracking sound is mine.

LESS FALLING

The young girls smell of cardamom, purple
sumac, pomegranate molasses and lemons.
They teach me words like Kunafe, let me taste
the syrup-soaked cheese pastry their mother made.
The girls tell me they remember the sounds
of bombs that made them shake but not hear,
the mortar shells that blasted concrete walls,
and crawling out from under the mattress
pulled off the bed. Sanaa, the older one,
says, *I always know where to hide.* Look,
I say, the trees forgot how to hold their leaves.
Jana is wiser. *Maybe they are tired and need
to rest.* The girls find a mitten on the playground
and move it between their four hands, taking turns
to keep warm. When winter came I promised them
snow. It hasn't fallen. Sanaa says, *Less falling
from the sky is fine with me.* Now they spin
the merry-go-round that nobody rides.

MOUNT ZION CEMETERY

Looking for mosquito larvae

stones upon stones, and on them, names
no one uses today, names like Dorothy
and Jeremiah, carved (not etched)
(maybe with a stick) in wet cement
tossed in a pile. Dead upon dead,
the ghosts who took up too much space
now regulated to the trash heap in the
cemetery. Walking in the grass grown
too high, I step on the bones
that have risen above ground,
skulls and clavicles holding water
so thick with mosquito larvae
I am compelled to empty the skeletons
and scatter them.

BUFFALO BAYOU

The bayou overflowed,
spread like a spilled glass of wine
and stained my sister's home.
The flood line rose on her walls
until it was time to go.
On a double kayak,
she floated in her house.
Beds glided, paintings swayed
as my sister paddled out the door
with her husband and two dogs
through water worth nothing.
Baby fish and water moccasins took over.
Have it, she said. *There's nothing we own.*
For five days the bayou overflowed
Until roofs disappeared and live oak
trees drowned. She returned
to warped tables, crumbling drywall,
and mattresses that took five men to move.
So little to save. Two Pyrex dishes, a gravy boat,
a Christmas cactus. Someday, it will bloom.
No grief breaks, she said. *We start over.*

Squirrels fatten on acorns

PORCINI

Tonight, the forest opens
as the rain ends. It's the kind
of weather my father loved.

I pack his curved knife
and woven basket to hunt
for squirrel's bread, the king

of mushrooms that tastes
like smoked stone
and flourishes as he does

in the dank and dark
under black pine trees.
I search for chestnut

brown umbrella heads,
fleshy white meat
with pores underneath.

I find them where I always
do in the soft earth.
Covered in worms, my father

Whispers, *work around them.*
Cut shallow on the stem.
Avoid the mycelium.

I kneel in the dirt,
unsheathe my blade
and slice.

BURIED IN TEXAS

Your wife buried you under
a Live Oak tree like the one
we played on as kids. I
wonder if you told her

how you hoisted me up
to the tree's valley of branches
and climbed up to meet me.
You pulled the licorice from your pocket.

We ate it all. You black, me red.
We swung our legs until our cowboy boots
flew off like torpedoes. With bare feet, we
climbed higher. Catch me, I said.

And you did. We sat in the tree blowing
smoke rings from the pipe you stole
from your father. You gave me
the silver necklace with a charm

shaped like the state of Texas. I'm at your
grave wearing the black dress, the one
with tiny purple flowers and the scalloped hem.
You would remember.

THE RUT

The doe leads the buck on a death
hunt tearing across cemetery grounds.
Dry leaves whirl back up into the sky
as she hurdles white tombstones and tramples
fresh graves. With one antler broken, he chases
her over the hurricane fence, into the parkway.

I lead you, too. I wear my red dress, curl
my hair, paint my lips and cheeks different
shades. You walk me to my car and ask if
you can follow me home. I navigate
through the dark, sometimes speeding up
to see if you will drive faster.

The doe's hoof clips my fender as she bounds
across the road and disappears into the woods
on the other side. From my rearview mirror
I watch the buck dive into your car. Broken
antler catches on the open window, spinning you both
in the other direction.

A HONEYMOON IN BALI

A 12-inch-long
purple and green
gecko clung to the wall
of our hotel bathroom,
scurried when I sat down.
Rather than battle with a reptile,
I took to the outside.
There's an element of bravery
peeing in the dark,
among bushes we did not know.
My husband and I,
we were in this together
for a while. He held my hands
as I squatted over an edge.
When the concierge walked by,
escorting another couple
to their room, the flashlight
glow settled on the white,
sweet-smelling gardenias
and my bare behind.

THE RAT CATCHER

He pedals along Hanoi's unlit streets. A bamboo
basket in back, filled with a lump of moving
gray, tilts his bicycle from side to side. Caged
rats climb over one another, testing

the man's balance as they look for a way out.
He stops, leans his bicycle onto the utility pole
and walks toward a hole in the street. Kneeling,
he places his mouth against the pavement

and extends one arm to set a net. A high-pitch
whistle sends the rats screeching out of the sewer
into his catch. He carries them toward the basket,
opens its hatch. Old bodies shift for the new.

WAITING IN TORNILLO

35 miles from El Paso
a Guatemalan girl
leans against a chain link fence
topped with barbed wire.
Seventy days waiting
in the midday sun
in a city of beige tents
staked in rock and dirt
the rumble of the generators
so loud it's hard to think
no mothers, no fathers
she braids stories
into the hair of her younger
sister. The last of 6,200
in the desert, the girl
sticks her fingers through the wire
shaped like steel diamonds.

LAUGHING WOMEN

Nanda is a vegetarian
only during the day
when she teaches salsa
dancing on the terrace
of her Delhi apartment
to women in fur hats
and bare feet. Overheated
women with no partners
laugh with their bangles
when they draw scolds
from gawking men.

*

Light pink curlers stand
perpendicular to her head.
Harlequin romance in hand,
she leans against the washer
hips gyrating with the spin.
The page never turns.
When the buzzer sounds her
husband retrieves the basket.
From washer to dryer they
move clothes together.

*

A motorcycle-riding,
watermelon growing Brazilian,
Sister Maria left her husband
in daylight. She bought a brothel
with a group of women. Sex sells,
so they create chocolate in
the shape of kama sutra positions
and peddle the candy to men
who pay to eat from them.

I LEFT MY GIRLFRIEND FOR MY WIFE

for Charles Bukowski

I want to fuck you, mary said.
Hand me my whiskey, I said.
No, I want to fuck you.

So we did.
Hand me a cigarette, I said.
I want to fuck again, mary said.

I've been shacking up with you
for seven years, mary.
I like to smoke and drink, I said.

and I left.
I walked to linda's apartment, it was small.
she was on the couch with her stomach

pouching the way a good drunk's belly
rises below the chest.
I would drink from you all day

if you let me, I said. she did.
we took two cold beers from the refrigerator
and sat back on the couch drinking

from one another's bottles.
let's fuck, hank, she said. we did.
we smoked, drank and fucked all night.

yeah, we did.

MEN

The bats roam the house
freely, when before
I chased them with a broom
and caught them in a paper bag.
I wear a shower cap
in the living room now,
dare them to confuse
my hair for a nest, like men.

THE SONG

This morning my love and I wake up in Lenin Park
in a bed of banana leaves. Skinny black chickens peck
at the crumbs we've left from our bánh mì.
A woman pumps her sugar cane wheel. We drink
the sweet juice and call it breakfast. My love
joins the shoeshine boys in their game
knocking Coke cans over. He throws his black dress shoe
into their heap of yellow plastic sandals and lets them win.
We walk to the Red River's brown water. He flags down
the woman with the motorboat and loads our bicycle. We float
away from the city to the village where his mother lives.
The boatwoman, she paddles, navigates us past water
buffaloes blowing bubbles. When we arrive downstream,
we unload our bike. I sit on the rack. He carries me
through rice fields. We weave on rutted paths.
His mother greets us in her rubber boots,
a bandana over her head. *Have you eaten yet?* she asks.
Before we answer, she says, *let's start with the dead.*
His five-year-old brother blew up in a landmine yesterday
while digging for gold she buried during the war.
She tells us this as if she's reading the newspaper.
His mother has forgotten how to mourn.
The clouds separate and rain barrels catch my grief.
She mixes coal powder with water, shapes it
to look like cow dung, slaps it to the wall for drying,
and sings *Mùa Thu Cho Em.*

THE LAS VEGAS HOTEL

Hanoi, Vietnam (1995)

I wash my clothes in the sink, hang
them to dry over my luggage and lie
on the bed naked watching Larry King Live.
Larry King, my new best friend.
With a bloated stomach full of phở,
it's too early to sleep. I wrap myself
in the red velour drapes and go to the roof
to watch the children fly their kites.
A boy holds a string. An old woman
in her conical hat works her way
down the laundry line. The clothes flap
in the wind, moving furiously toward dry.
One shirt balloons and flies off, flutters
back and forth like a boat on Hồ Tây.
The arms wrap around the bodice,
twisting the shirt into a ball. I
lean into the air to catch it.
A cape of red soars behind me.

YELLOWSTONE

At least five times my size   maybe more

    I was never good at approximating

in that contained space   this cow was so much bigger

    when I walked out of the bathroom stall

her back was to me   I don't think she noticed me at all

    so fixated   she was on herself   those brown eyes stared

she turned her neck slightly   to see the back of her head

    how did her spindly legs hold   I pressed myself

against the tiled walls   if she kicked   I'd be telling

    a different story   mosquitoes flew by her ears

she shook them off   I wondered if   she admired herself

    often a reflection   so beautiful

pockets of green leaves

HA LONG BAY

The rusted cargo ferry carried us from Hai Phong
to Ha Long Bay where limestone mountains rise
from emerald waters. The captain let us dive off
the top deck into the deep. Giant mushroom-

shaped jellyfish floated toward us.
We swam through caves and climbed
the karst rock that put holes in our hands.
Tired, we leaned back into the warm sea.

PREGNANT IN VIENTIANE

I live in one of those fancy white houses
with the orange-tiled roofs, outside of town
across from the cows that graze in the yard
filled with coconut trees. The monks roam
past in their yellow robes. I set up a badminton
net but they never want to play. They say
poisonous snakes like the grass. Sometimes we
ride together in a Tuk Tuk toward town to buy water.
In the mornings before the ash from burning trash
takes over the air, I walk on the dirt paths between
the rice paddies that lead me to the temple
where Buddhist monks speak.

SUNNY DAYS

(September 11, 2001–Arlington, Virginia)

7:00 a.m.
My husband wakes me
with a kiss I won't remember
for years. It's beautiful outside.
He feeds breakfast to our daughter.

7:20 a.m.
I hold her three-year-old hand as we walk
to the park. She wears ladybug sandals.
I push her in the swing, catch her at
the bottom of the slide. She asks, did God exist
before dinosaurs? Why do we have chins?

8:00 a.m.
Momma, on sunny days,
does God like us more? Does God like us
at the exact time we do bad things?
Momma, if God is so special,
why don't we have God toys?

9:30 a.m.
I lie on the couch. She plays dolls,
uses my pregnant belly as a stage.

EPISTLE

Back when people used to write letters,
standing in the post office line, I said
to the man in front of me, I want to
eat my baby, the one I am holding.
I licked her toes and told him
I knew it wasn't normal, but she
belonged back inside my body.
I held her foot and showed him
how large my mouth opened, like the gators
in the bayou. It would take just one swallow.

RECESS

Like a starfish, arms and legs splayed out,
my daughter asks me to draw her in purple.
From the chalk box, I grab lavender
and outline her body.

At four, her fingers still don't open wide enough.
She wiggles when my hand brushes her skin.
Be still, like a dead man.
She asks, "Do dead men sing in heaven?"

Yes, it's the sound of coyotes howling.
Don't move. The chalk is smearing.
She stiffens her whole self,
and I finish filling her in.

Let's see how big you are.
I lean down and hold each hand.
She jumps out of her body
and turns to face her shape.

SCIENTISTS' CLIFFS, MARYLAND

Bald eagles swoop over
Chesapeake Bay
one side, ocean, open sky
the other, humid forest
where moss grows on
elevated boardwalks that run
through the tree canopy
wooden staircases lead us
from cliffs to beach
crowded with rotting logs
discarded by the sea.
I hunt for shark teeth
black fossil washed
up with shells. My daughters
float in inner tubes, loop
arms and legs together
bob on the waves.
I scout for jellyfish.
The Lion's mane
evades my protection
wraps its tentacles around us
like fishing lines.
Today, this is our biggest problem.
We don't know about tomorrow.
So we stay out of the water
march through the woods
pretend we are queens
sit in a circle threading colored string
sing off key, recite to one
another from memory.

11-YEAR-OLD

Her turquoise robe flying
behind her like a cape,
she runs. Cars move past her
on their way home from work.
She swings her arms back
and forth like her father taught her
so she can run faster, hoping
the cape will lift her into the sky
away from me.

TAROT

1. *The Magician*
I drove my daughters to rural Virginia
to watch me jump out of an airplane.
Chloe and Cynthia needed to believe we could be
happy. Their dad was getting married. I wanted
my girls to stop worrying.
At 10 and 13 years old,
they did not want a step-mother.
Not until I was suited in my harness
did I think about alternative outcomes.
What if the chute didn't open?
As I kissed them goodbye
they were excited
about the stories they would tell.

2. *The Fool*
I climbed into the one-propeller
plane and sat on a long wooden bench.
The ground, my daughters, moved away.
When it was my turn, I sat on the floor.
My legs hung out the open door.
I don't remember jumping just
falling, facing the earth.
I thought the Shenandoah Valley
looked as it always does–
rounded hills worn out
no sharp edges like those
younger mountains in the West.

3. *The Lovers*
I never felt the adrenaline
until after I bruised my tailbone.
It was the same with my marriage.
On our way home, we passed
a sign on the highway.
"Readings by Jasmine."
We did a U-turn.
The psychic was as we wanted–
a purple flowery dress, red scarf
tied in her hair. Her cigarette
teetered on a pink lotus ashtray,
smoke floated to the ceiling
where seven disco balls twirled.

4. *The Tower*
Jasmine told Cynthia not to worry.
She would get married and never divorce.
Chloe would marry someone with an accent.
The girls were happy and it cost only $35.
So I went back. The second time I grew bitter
about the three-hour drive, the gas,
and the $75 special: tarot cards, numerology
and love readings. My ex-husband was married.
I swore I wouldn't return. The third time,
the highway sign was covered over.
I drove up Jasmine's gravel drive.
The door was boarded up with a giant X.
I thought about knocking.

VICUÑA

Working in Bolivia

In the Andes five hours from the road that splits in two
where the quinoa blooms maroon, the blind boy falls
asleep near the coal stove. His sister stands next to me as
I offer her mother a safer way of cooking. In Quechuan,
the mother says, "The eyes go first. Then the lungs."
A dried fetal vicuña–a good luck charm–hangs
from the ceiling. It cost $700, three years' of her income.
Three years of not sending her children to school.
The dead animal spins in rhythm with the wind,
faster, she says, when the luck is good. She smiles through
the smoke that keeps us warm. My phone buzzes.
"Mom, please come home." Her daughter looks the same age
as mine. I've been gone all winter. Three months working,
three months not keeping my child warm. Her chapped hands
bleed the color of quinoa. I lean back into her daughter.

YEARS LATER

What would the perfect day look like?
I asked you.
Simple, you said.
No stairs to climb, the sun is shining.
I dragged
the mattress to the living room
and placed it
near the oversized bay windows.
You watched
daffodils bloom in their pots
before Easter
and dictated letters to your other daughter.
We sorted
tea cups and marked the giveaways.
In the afternoons
I read *Lonesome Dove* aloud to you.
Before you slept,
I wiped your face, your feet, your arms, your legs.

SERVICE

They know which dresses to wear. We had four funerals
last year. Some we are still mourning. For the first time
in months, my daughters sit on the front stoop, laughing.
Chloe's play opens today; Cynthia has a soccer game.
Mother is dying. I wonder if she would mind waiting
a week, two at the most. I promised her a beautiful service,
one people will remember. The doctors can manage her pain.
Maybe it's not as bad as I imagine. We will read the prayers,
the scriptures she underlined in her King James.
I will give her the open-casket funeral she wanted,
if she grants me this favor.

GEODES

I take my daughters back
to the Texas Hill Country.
We eat with the same stars

as my mother and I once did.

We pull the corn husks
from our tamales, dip the insides
in chili sauce and sour cream.

We walk the same riverbed,
skip flat stones into dark
and hunt for geodes.

I remember her saying

Look for the crystal rocks.
They are rounder and lighter than others.
Chisel them, and they open.

I'VE ALWAYS WANTED TO BE

a Kwanzan cherry tree
exploding recklessly into spring.

No one ever tells her
Your blooms are too much.

Does she feel loss
when her flushed petals leave?

She spits out oxygen for anyone.
Is there a way to seal my mouth over her?

It's not all I want.

With years, she peels back her skin.
No apologies. They all still come.

Cardinals land on knotted limbs
like a child once climbed on me.

I remember planting magenta impatiens,
my newborn in yellow blankets by my side.

I wore the green-checked dress
my mother sewed.

I believed to be happier would be impossible.

ABOUT DAY EIGHT

This book was produced by the non-profit Day Eight. Day Eight's mission is to empower individuals and communities to participate in the arts through the production, publication, and promotion of creative projects. Our vision is to be part of the healing of the world through the arts. Day Eight's programming includes an online magazine, poetry events, live arts programming, book publishing, education programs for children and youth, and activities to support arts journalism.

Example 2020 projects:

The DC Arts Writing Fellowship was created to support early career arts writers. Day Eight recently received a multi-year funder commitment to expand the project, which works in partnership with local news outlets Tagg Magazine, DC Theatre Scene, and The DC Line.

The DC Poet Project is a poetry reading series and open-to-all poetry competition that supports DC area poets. The project functions through partnerships with the DC Public Library, Anacostia Coordinating Council, and Brink Media. The spring 2020 DC Poet Project was produced through support from the Wells Fargo Community Foundation and the National Endowment for the Arts.

Day Eight's local art history work includes an online archive dedicated to DC's first artist cooperative gallery. An Advisory Board of community members including arts and museum professionals oversee and support Day Eight's art history projects.

Day Eight's projects are made possible by the dedicated support of volunteers and individual donors, including the Board of Directors. To join us visit www.DayEight.org.

Day Eight

Ship To:

Kim Baxter
3626 N LANCASTER ST
ARLINGTON, VA 22207-1334

Order ID: 113-5708632-6663461

Thank you for buying from Day Eight on Amazon Marketplace.

Shipping Address:	Order Date:	Mon, Oct 26, 2020
Kim Baxter	Shipping Service:	Standard
3626 N LANCASTER ST	Buyer Name:	Kim
ARLINGTON, VA 22207-1334	Seller Name:	Day Eight

Quantity	Product Details	Unit price	Order Totals
1	**Just One Swallow [Paperback] [2020] Laura P. McCarty** **SKU:** HH-R98B-YLAN **ASIN:** 0999078046 **Condition:** New **Listing ID:** 0921XUKGC9V **Order Item ID:** 51807577590330	$18.00	**Item subtotal** $18.00 **Shipping total** $3.99 **Tax** $1.32 **Item total** **$23.31**

Grand total: $23.31

Go to "Your Account" on Amazon.com, click "Your Orders" and then click the "seller profile" link for this order to get information about the return and refund policies that apply.
Visit https://www.amazon.com/returns to print a return shipping label. Please have your order ID ready.

Thanks for buying on Amazon Marketplace. To provide feedback for the seller please visit www.amazon.com/feedback. To contact the seller, go to Your Orders in Your Account. Click the seller's name under the appropriate product. Then, in the "Further Information" section, click "Contact the Seller."